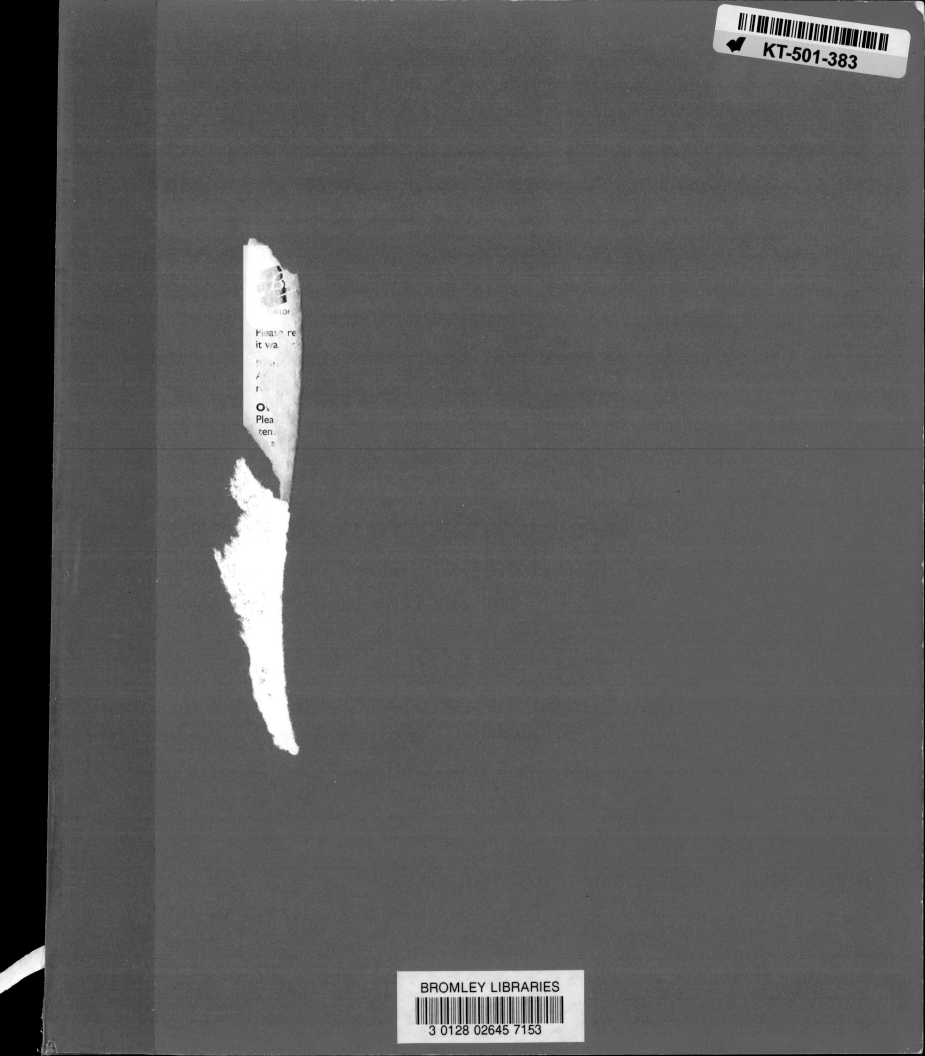

IDEAS FOR LIVING

IDEAS FOR LIVING

styling tips and solutions for every room

Foreword by Ali Hanan

Foreword

If our homes were people they would find it hard to live up to our expectations. We want them to be stylish, but also functional. We want them to be clean-lined and modern, but full of character. We clutter them with our things, yet we yearn for space. It's a tough, thankless job being a modern home.

No wonder our homes can often seem a little unloved. Yet these spaces are the backdrop to our lives. Every room bears witness to our milestones and minutiae. And it's not just about us. We come with our entourage of extended family, fickle children, drop-in friends and busy-body pets who all have their own demands. It's not surprising a home finds it hard to balance chaos and order, and comfort and style.

Enter *Ideas for Living*, which takes you by the hand and shows you how to create a home where you – and your family – can really live. Visiting each room in the home, one by one, it highlights the questions you need to address when planning, decorating and organizing your interior, and gives suggestions and practical ideas to help you find the ideal solution for your own home. Many interiors books make homes look like perfect still lifes. And while showroom homes are beautiful to admire, they aren't grounded in the reality of a 'working' house. All of the homes in this book, however, live, breathe, function and evolve like real families do. They know what it's like to be everything to everyone – and still look stylish.

Ideas for Living gives you advice on how to create a home that's useful, hard-working and still looks alluring. It shows you how to accommodate children's and parents' needs, old heirloom pieces and modern looks, work and leisure, technology and nature, and gain comfort without sacrificing style. This hands-on book will help you to create a harmonious interior that suits all of its inhabitants – and your home, too. Use it to help you turn your living space into a real home for you and your family to live in and love. Your home will thank you.

Ali Hanan

Contents

Wish lists Every room in your home makes its own demands. Similarly, everyone who lives there has his or her own ideas on how things should be. The way we arrange a home reflects the different phases in our lives and our varying desires and needs for each room. This book neatly addresses these needs. Each chapter begins with a wish list. In the pages that follow, we will show you how to turn these wishes into reality.

Room by room All of the rooms found in your home are dealt with in the following eight chapters: beginning with the entrance and making your way through the hall and corridor, the living room and kitchen, the bedroom and bathroom, children's rooms, working space and the attic. We provide ideas for every space – on how to furnish, arrange, organize and decorate. Photographs and layouts are supplied, together with explanations and hints.

Your own home *Ideas for Living* shows you how to make your home exciting, stylish and contemporary; how to keep it neat, practical and organized; how to arrange each room as efficiently as possible and decorate attractively; how to combine old items with new ones; and how to make your home comfortable and give it character.

Chapter 1

Entrance

Come in! Enter a warm, cheerful hallway, move through a welcoming corridor, up an inviting staircase, onto a stylish landing ... This 'public space' is a foretaste of the rest of your home. It should invite you in and enfold you. Welcome!

Making a personal statement on how you live begins at the front door

de jassen kast

Ben om vijf uur thuis!

Wish list:

- *ambience*
- *good cloakroom*
- *notes for the family*
- *getting rid of clutter*
- *light*
- *colour*

What do we want from a hall, a staircase, a landing or a corridor? Usually, not much – to hang up a coat properly, to get rid of a bag or a pair of wellingtons, or an umbrella, to be able to make your way through without too much obstruction. No more than that. The 'public space' in our homes is often the poor relation when compared with other rooms. And this is a shame, as this space is more than the place where we wipe our feet, take off our jackets and 'move on through' to another room.

It is where we come in and immediately sense the aura of a home. It is where we gain a first impression of who lives there, which is why it is a good idea for the space to express warmth, and why it is the ideal place to create something special in your own taste and style.

Anyone drawing up a wish list soon realizes the variety of things that can actually be included in an entrance hall or corridor. Prudent organization, choosing a particular colour and clever lighting can all make a significant difference. What's more, a great deal is possible even in a small area: practical coat-hanging space, a central notice board for the family and creative solutions for 'wasted' spaces. Make the entrance at least as inviting as the living room. As soon as you come inside and the door shuts behind you, you should feel immediately at home.

!idea

Aim to create a tidy entrance hall with imaginative ideas: store boots on a shelf; keep items for sport and other leisure activities in bags; and write the family's daily movements on a plate of glass with erasable felt pens.

idea

Echo the style used in the living room in the hall. The key in this country family home is a casual, warm ambience combined with practicality. Notice how the red front door is painted white on the inside to create additional light.

Ambience

To give the entrance hall or corridor its own character, think of this space in the same way as you would a living room, and choose colours, materials and a style that you like. A hall that is decorated in an elegant, classical style is a world away from a cosy hall in a practical family home, as in the photograph opposite. Yet both halls say something about the owners because they have been decorated with just as much attention as the rest of the house and contain elements that will be encountered again elsewhere: a curtain in a particular colour, a rug (machine washable) and pictures on the wall. This helps you to feel immediately at home as soon as you step indoors.

Good cloakroom

Where do you leave your coat? Coat hooks or pegs on the wall are useful in narrow passageways. And they don't always have to be arranged in a horizontal row. You could cover the wall with them, from floor to ceiling. Pegs lower down can be used for holding bags or children's coats; the higher pegs are ideal for things you use less often. If you prefer to hang up coats on hangers, you must find space for a strong rail from which to hang them. The perfect spot is between two walls; you could even build a false wall. A shelf placed above this for accessories creates a harmonious picture. Coats can hang in built-in cupboards, completely out of view behind closed doors. This sort of furniture is not usually planned for the hall, but it is no bad idea if the width of the space allows; this will give you acres of closet space for all those things which are normally just lying about.

Notes for the family

Who has gone where, and when will they be back? What do you need to buy, and who has gone to buy it? And what do you have to remember at all costs? The entrance hall and corridor are ideal places to post notes, timetables and assorted messages for all the family. There are countless options to consider for such a notice board. For example, a simple version can be made by painting corkboard in a fun colour or covering it in fabric. A plate of glass can be written on with erasable felt pen, or you could use a sheet of metal or zinc, with magnets and spaces for each day of the week or for each member of the family. A surface can be painted with blackboard paint (now also available in colours other than black), or you could use a batten, to which you screw bulldog clips to hold any letters and receipts that you might otherwise misplace.

"Being at home makes me happy."

!idea

Left: dare to experiment. Instead of using a rail for your coat hangers, install a broad, 'suspended' shelf with special hooks on the underside. You can store accessories and personal items on the shelf. Right: photographs and magazine cuttings help to make your hall unlike any other.

Getting rid of clutter

You can keep the hall tidy but still create a cosy, lived-in feel. Unsightly clutter should be concealed behind doors and in boxes, but interesting and attractive items can be displayed. Keys, scarves and other items that lie around can be stored away neatly in wicker baskets for a rustic-look hall or in aluminium boxes for a more modern look. Put up hooks and hang ready-made bags on the wall for music, sports and other leisure equipment; use handwritten labels for boxes and baskets; allocate hooks or pegs to each member of the family, with their names next to them. The hall will look more unified if boxes and baskets are kept in one style or colour.

Light

The hall and corridor are often confined, dark spaces. The lighter they are, the roomier they appear. Let as much daylight as possible stream indoors, and reflect this light using mirrors and pale-coloured surfaces. Another possibility is to paint everything in one pale colour and the inside of the front door white. Electric lighting in the hall or corridor should be more than an obligatory, solitary ceiling lamp. Light has to be functional, of course – there is nothing worse than fishing out two left-hand gloves from a drawer in the dark – but why not treat light in the hall in the same way that you would in the living room? Well-chosen lighting puts life and energy into your hall. To keep several different lighting sources in one hall practical, arrange for all of them to be turned on, off or dimmed from one light switch. And if you still want just one ceiling lamp, remember that the plainest corridor can be enlivened with a special light fixture, such as a chandelier or Moroccan-style lamp with coloured glass.

Colour

We are only ever in the hall for a short time, so this is the space above all others for colour experimentation. If you feel that a completely red living room is rather too much of a good thing in practice, you can still follow your heart's desire by having a red hallway. One wall in a strong colour is enough to create a powerful effect. Cooler colours, such as shades of blue, create space because they give the illusion of depth. Warmer colours, such as red and orange, make a space appear a little smaller, but create a cosier atmosphere. If your hall is roomy, consider introducing green in the form of leafy houseplants. If you are displaying photographs, cuttings and paintings, you can alter the hall's colour tones by changing the items from time to time.

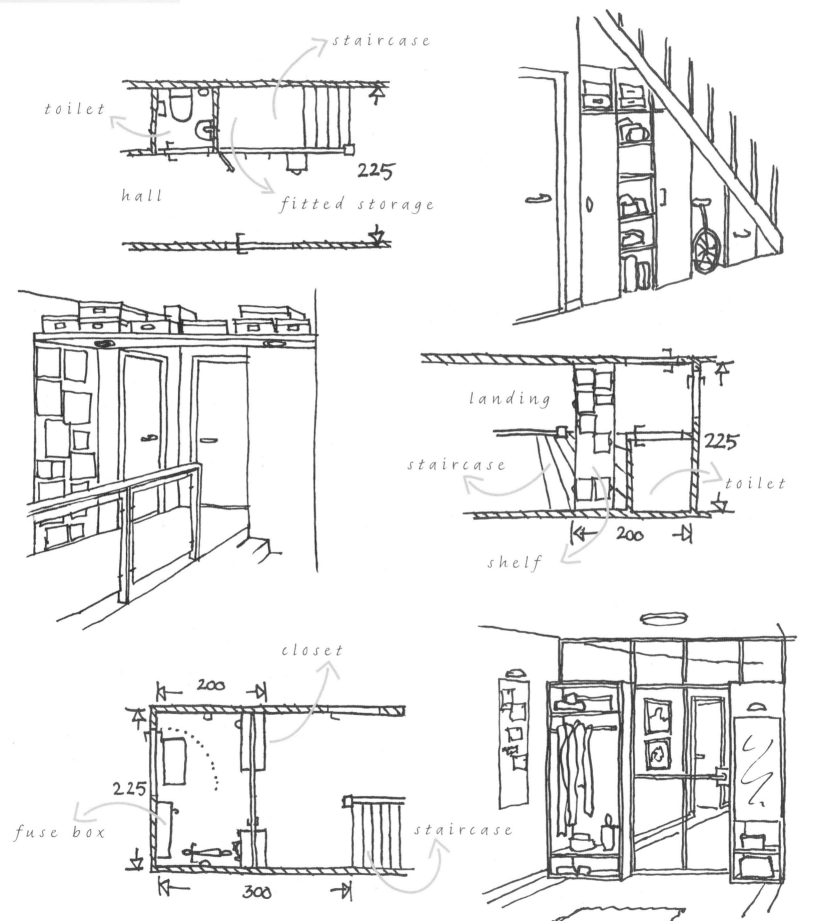

staircase

toilet

hall

fitted storage

225

landing

staircase

225

toilet

200

shelf

closet

200

225

fuse box

300

staircase

Entrance layout

The hall, corridor and landing are ideal places for solving the problem of clutter. If you have a large space, erect a glass-and-metal partition wall across the centre of the hall, with a closet and storage cupboard to the left and right. Use the space under the stairs to tidy away sports items, bicycles, suitcases and the vacuum cleaner. Or create a false ceiling that acts as a sturdy storage shelf.

Chapter 2

Living space

While living is something we do wherever we are in the house, we associate it particularly with the living room because the space is for everybody. It is where we relax, eat, read, watch television, throw parties … It is where our lives intermingle.

Talking, laughing, being together: life in all its variety is played out in the living room

Wish list

- seating
- eating
- television
- walls
- organization
- light
- greenery

The living room is the nerve centre of your home – it is where everyone gathers and where we are constantly busy doing anything and everything. It is a place for socializing and concentration, for commotion and relaxation. It is a place to be alone or a place to be together as a group. It is where we want to be able to sit, eat, watch television, work and much more besides. In fact, we want to be able to do any number of things in the living room, sometimes all at the same time.

Therefore the biggest question is: how to split up the space in a way that best caters to all of these multiple functions? Some clever rules of thumb can be utilized in order to accomplish this, but you should ask yourself a few essential questions first. What are your and your family's typical habits? Do you want an open space or private areas? What are your requirements for a dining table or living-room furniture? Where is the television going? Do you have any special plans for the walls? And what about the lighting? Do you want to give up some space for plants and flowers?

Only once you have the answers to these questions – once you know what you want and what you need – should the following issues be tackled: colour, style and layout. Your line of approach should be what feels best for you, regardless of how it is 'supposed' to be.

idea

It is best to choose a style based on your personality and current lifestyle. Do you need peace and harmony? Pale tones and natural wood create equilibrium in the midst of a hectic life; quiet as a counterbalance to clamour.

Seating

To **prevent the room looking crammed to the gills**, it is always best to stick to **similar colour tones**.

idea

Use the space so that you feel most comfortable. **Forget convention:** if sitting in the sun makes you happy, then put the chaise longue right next to the window.

!idea *A few armchairs instead of a sofa*

Personalized seating

Where is the best light for reading? Where do you feel most comfortable sitting: on the sofa, stretched out, or at the table? Where does the natural light come from and where can you sit blissfully in the sun? Sometimes you have to break with convention when working out seating areas. Rely on your feelings. It might result in you discovering a solitary relaxation and reading spot when you put the chaise longue next to the window. Or it might be a sprawling family sofa without any neighbouring armchairs. Or you might decide on only armchairs and no sofa because, after all, a sofa is not obligatory.

Your own space: a room en suite

The living room as one large, open space has long been seen as the ideal: the 'open plan' idea. Funnily enough, many people are now turning away from this. Following a period in which many sliding doors were removed, the traditional living room en suite is making a comeback. This is not as odd as it may sound: it is great to be able to screen yourself off from one half of the room, while still having the feeling that you are not completely shut off from everything in the other half. You can arrange a room to be like this even without sliding doors, creating two completely different and separate seating areas that are, for example, 'for activity' and 'for relaxation'. You could even use a tall shelf unit to form a zoning boundary as shown in the photograph on the left. By clearly giving each area a unique style or colour, you emphasize the room's dual functionality.

idea

A modern room en suite does not have to be divided by classic lattice or louvred doors. These sliding doors are made from **reclaimed wood**, as are the bookcases behind which the doors can be rolled.

idea If your heart's desire is a large sofa, go for something really big. **Dare to choose** extra-large, perhaps

Whether sprawled out or snuggling up, there is room for everyone here

modular furniture for different possible arrangements. Rule of thumb: very large sofas require no neighbouring chairs.

Eating

Make your dining table the heart of your home, a place where everyone can pull up a chair with a mug of coffee, refuel, chat or dissolve into laughter. The dining table deserves to be a focal point – in the middle of the room with a view on to the garden, perhaps, or opposite a fireplace – because eating together is what living together is all about.

There should always be room for unexpected guests. Pull up a chair!

idea

Take your cue from the light: put the dining table where the sun shines. Do you want to have breakfast in sunlight, or would you rather it was lunch or dinner? Think about this when making your decision, then organize the rest of your layout according to the table's position.

The dining table
The most popular dining table is spacious, long, wooden and rectangular in shape. Probably because it seems to offer an open invitation to sit down at it and because there is always room for one more. It is also conducive for doing different things at different times: eating, working, playing, reading the paper. It is perfectly OK for a table like this to look just that little bit well used and well loved. And it is perfectly OK to keep things on it. After all, this table is a focal point for life. A long, rectangular table fits in all sorts of spaces: you can divide a room in two by placing it with the short side next to a wall; putting it in the centre creates a dominant feature. If you prefer the latter, you might consider getting a round table. Eight people can fit easily round a table 1.4m (4ft 6in) in diameter. The advantage is that you can look each other in the eye more easily and avoid missing out on conversations going on at opposite ends of the table. By the way, who says that a dining table has to be at chair height and imposing? If you prefer eating informally on the sofa or in front of the television, then a seating arrangement with a lower, smaller table might be the perfect solution for you.

Dining chairs
Most people choose the table first, then the chairs, but you could do it the other way round. What do you want from your dining chairs? Comfort? Elegance? Easy to wipe clean? Some people spend such a long time at the table, or do so many different things there, that they prefer to use armchairs; others get pleasure from rustic, wooden stools because they match their style better. For comfort and good posture, you could use stylish ergonomically designed office chairs. Or, you could combine simple chairs with rather more up-market ones. One fun idea is to have chairs that are all different. You can still create a harmonious effect if you choose the same upholstery, or paint them all the same colour. Or perhaps you could have chairs on one side and a bench with no backrest on the other. This makes it easy to slip in an extra person.

You can fit many more chairs around a round table than a traditional four-sided one. Plus it is easier to talk to each other.

idea The 'canteen' look for a big family dinner. The adults sit on one side (on chairs).

On the other side, the children can happily slide along (on the bench).

Light above the table

Nothing dictates the ambience and defines the style in an eating area as much as the lighting used above the dining table. A new light or lamp can reinvigorate the entire space, but it is hard to find and choose the perfect lamp. After all, a light above a table also has to serve a practical function. Take time to consider all the uses you have for your table. Do people work or read at it? If so, it is important to have bright reading light. Then again, that sort of light is probably too intense for an intimate dinner, so it might be a good idea to install a dimmer switch to allow you to adjust the light according to the situation. It can look stylish to have two or three lamps in a row, instead of one in the middle. A row of three chandeliers, for example, can look both elegant and festive, if this suits your interior (and it does not have to be a traditional one; in fact, the contrast between a heavy table and a decorative chandelier can be quite startling). If light to work by is not essential, there is nothing to stop you from deciding to do without a lamp above the table altogether and instead putting in place one or more candlesticks for daily romantic meals by candlelight.

The details

What you need to set the table – tablecloths, napkins, crockery, cutlery – does not have to be a style unto itself. Choose crockery that suits your interior and display it in a cabinet or on a shelf or dresser next to the dining table. Coordinate the colour(s) of your dinner service and table linen with the colour(s) used elsewhere in the room, or vice versa. It is useful if your dining table incorporates a drawer in which to store day-to-day cutlery, placemats and other tableware (or coloured pencils, paper and the like if you also use the table as a work or play space). The more 'kitchen-oriented' the dining area within a living room is, the more informal it looks. Some people who have kitchen–diners find that they hardly ever use their living rooms.

! idea

Mixing styles creates a self-confident, contemporary effect: masculine director's chairs with refined tableware; **sunny ochre-yellow** walls with classic pleated lampshades.

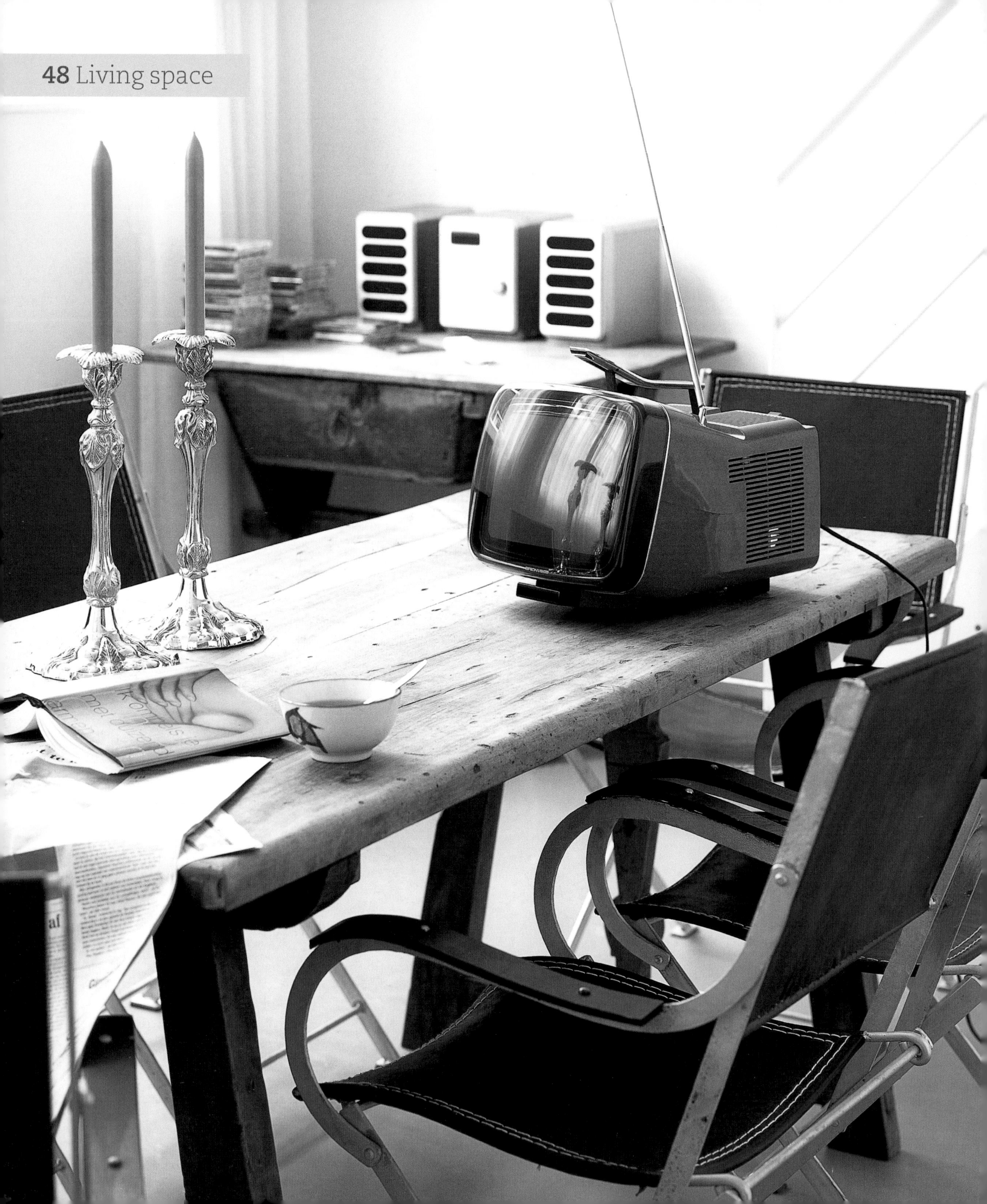

The television

Hands up those who have a love–hate relationship with their television. Not everyone at once! It may be a faithful member of the family, but at times it is also a noisy, ugly thing that competes with attractive furnishings and quiet areas. Should it be the focal point of a room? Should you have it on view? Or should it be hidden away when not in use?

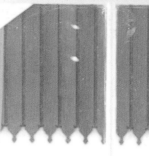

! idea

Investing in a television with an attractive design can remove a big source of irritation: the latest flatscreen models are great to look at, even when the television is switched off. Two chaise longues allow you the option either to watch television or to turn your back on it.

Not dominant, but in

harmony with everything else

The conspicuous television

The newest televisions – and other electronic equipment – are becoming ever more glamorous in design. In fact, the television can even be a bonus for your interior in terms of enhancing its style. If so, then let it be conspicuous. What are your family's viewing habits? If everyone at home watches a lot of television, it makes sense to give it a central position. This also makes it worthwhile purchasing something special, such as a flatscreen or designer television in the colour or style of your interior. If you have space for a separate television area in the living room or beyond it, consider building one in so that everyone who wants to watch can do so, and those who don't are not bothered by it.

The inconspicuous television

Perhaps you watch television very little and see it as an ugly piece of equipment. In that case, keep it behind closed doors. You do not have buy a ready-made television console (this can often take on the look of a modern-day altarpiece); a deep cabinet with adequate ventilation serves just as well – if necessary, remove the back. You might also consider using a computer console with doors or a low cabinet on casters. If the television is to remain on view, there are ways to make it less conspicuous. Choose a colour so that it blends with its surroundings – or, more easily, the other way round. Place accessories next to it that deflect attention away from it as a focal point, such as a painting, artwork or plant.

idea !

Do not turn the television, VCR and stereo system into a tower of objects. Also, putting something next to the TV that is larger than it, such as a tall plant or a painting, makes it less imposing.

Walls

It is no exaggeration to say that walls form the basis of our home's interior. Whether they are neutral tones or strikingly coloured, strewn with personal photographs, cuttings, drawings and paintings, or even turned into blackboards, our walls are decorated in a way that makes us feel comfortable. They are the backdrop to our lives.

Paint

The fastest way to create a new effect in a room is by changing the paint. A single wall can be painted an eye-catching colour in just one afternoon. And if you decide you don't like it, another colour can easily cover your mistake. Having one wall in a bright colour, while leaving the rest white, also creates a lively ambience. However, working with contrasting shades of the same colour can be just as effective. If you are hesitant to strike out with bold colours, try painting something else in that colour first, such as the inside of an open-fronted cupboard, as in the photograph on the left. Play with extremes, and create contrasts between what you hang on the wall and the colour you paint it – white picture frames against dark backgrounds, for example.

Wallpaper

Wallpaper gives you the opportunity to work with special patterns and textures. Many patterns are romantic, such as *toile de jouy* (opposite, below right) or other floral or plant designs. Instead of combining pretty designs such as these with a 'dainty' interior, use them against more masculine furnishings, coarser materials and simpler, more austere shapes. Striped wallpaper accentuates a room's height (vertical) or its length (horizontal). The same principle applies to wallpaper as to paint: you do not have to paper every wall. Just one wall with a strong motif can give a room a complete facelift.

Blackboard

Blackboard paint turns a wall into a playful, constantly changing element. You can use the wall for notes, shopping lists or reminders. Or you could create an artwork that changes regularly. Apply blackboard paint to a sheet of MDF, then hang it in place. Or cover an entire wall or even just part of it with paint – the wall must be level and smooth. Nowadays, blackboard paint is available in a variety of colours as well as black: do you fancy red or fuchsia pink?

Wood

You could choose wood or laminates to cover your walls – and not necessarily in the form of traditional panelling, but in large sheets or veneer. In the room shown opposite, above left, an aura of country house elegance was created by gluing American walnut veneer to sheets of MDF.

Walls set the tone more than furniture or lighting. Want a new style? Start with the walls.

idea You do not necessarily have to decorate the walls with paintings or photographs. You could decide to use graphics, with the motifs based on **letters sawn from wood**.

idea A framed sheet of MDF, finished with **blackboard paint**, is as decorative as it is functional. The frame seen here is **especially deep** to allow items to rest on it.

!idea

What you hang on your walls is an expression of your personality, your life and your experiences. Nothing makes your house so uniquely yours as surrounding yourself with the things you love most. It is important to spend time on how you hang something and where you put it.

Picture frames

If you are someone who values photographs, art or other precious decorations for your walls, you may like to collect a variety of picture frames in different styles and materials. Frames can add visual appeal to even the simplest photograph or drawing. Alternatively, a wall covered with the same style of frame creates rhythm and adds authority to a living room. Framed black-and-white photographs are a classic look. If you have a good colour photograph, you could copy this in black and white on glossy or extra-thick paper to create a timeless, elegant effect. Don't hesitate to group images together. Framed pictures set alongside each other create calm and harmony; they can have an unsettling effect when spread apart across a wall in isolation.

No frames

You don't have to frame everything. In theory, you can put anything on the wall that creates an atmosphere or mood, however you choose do it. Hanging something up without a frame, if necessary using a simple drawing pin or stainless-steel nail, displays courage and character. Objects to choose for this treatment should have a distinctive appearance or unique design. And preferably they should be items that have a particular emotional attachment for you.

Organization

People behave like squirrels and magpies: there seems to be no end to what we will hoard or bring into our homes. Before you know it, it turns into a mountain of clutter. So where are we to put these things? On shelves or in chests? In boxes or display cases? In full view or out of sight? Time to look at some well-organized solutions!

idea

A display cabinet for books creates a **composed sense of order**. Let art books with **impressive covers face the room** and act like 'paintings'.

Books on view

Naturally, books are not clutter, but they can give that impression when left lying around all over the house, which is, of course, why we put them in bookcases. While this could be a standard bookcase, there are many other possibilities. It is customary to assemble all the books in a house in one place, instead of distributing them throughout. This soon produces the effect of an imposing library. A custom-made bookcase, from floor to ceiling, creates a sense of symmetry and orderliness. Cabinets that were originally intended for something else can sometimes be surprisingly appropriate for books. How about an attractive display cabinet, where you can keep your best books free of dust behind glass? In the photograph on the opposite page, separate seating has been placed next to a display cabinet like this, allowing people to browse and read at their leisure. Creating the feeling of a library really does not take all that much effort.

Books out of view

We are used to having books on view and arranging them in rows, but it might be that you do not feel the need to have their spines on view all the time. In that case, they can be placed behind closed doors in a cabinet; or in a chest or sideboard with deep drawers so that the spines can face upwards to make each title easily identifiable. Another original solution is to store books in transparent or translucent boxes. It keeps them tidy and dust-free, while still giving them a presence to some degree. An organizer with creative flair might even want to sort out books according to the colours of their spines.

idea

A sideboard with deep drawers makes a great storage space for all those things that you want to keep out of sight. It's suitable for books, too.

idea Fitted cabinets along an entire wall, even built around a door, make optimum use of space and are at the same time less imposing in a room. You can conceal a mountain of things behind all these doors.

What do you want to see?

If you want a tidy, clutter-free living room, the best thing to consider is which of your things it is essential for you to have surrounding you and in full view. This will force you to think properly about the style and character of your home. What do you find attractive and what is precious to you? Those things can go in a display cabinet or be reserved space on a shelf – neatly stacked, grouped together according to style or colour, or alternatively as solitary items in a special spot. In this way you can show off your precious items to their best advantage, rather than spreading them randomly throughout a room. Things that you cannot avoid keeping out on view because you need to have them where they are easily to hand look much better when displayed in neat piles or arranged thoughtfully.

What do you not want to see?

Any things that you do not want to see can be stored away in boxes or baskets, or behind doors. Choose cabinets that have doors or drawers so you can store things away neatly and find them easily. CDs that you want to play but do not need to see can be housed in cabinets with narrow shelving and sliding doors. Magazines and newspapers suit (transparent) boxes or baskets, or even a drawer. Invest in boxes, baskets and other containers that are aesthetically pleasing and suit your interior's style and colour. This could be anything from a collection of antique chests or a range of rustic wicker baskets to large, white boxes with metallic fittings, or simply a collection of old tins.

idea

Three 'hollow' planks on the wall can provide as much storage space as a cabinet, but are less imposing. You can make them yourself from untreated, unvarnished wood, or you could use CD display units instead.

idea

The trick is to find boxes that fit the shelf depth precisely – once put in place, the effect is quite startling. And if you have had enough of boxes on shelves, you can just put them somewhere else (stacked up perhaps): a movable library!

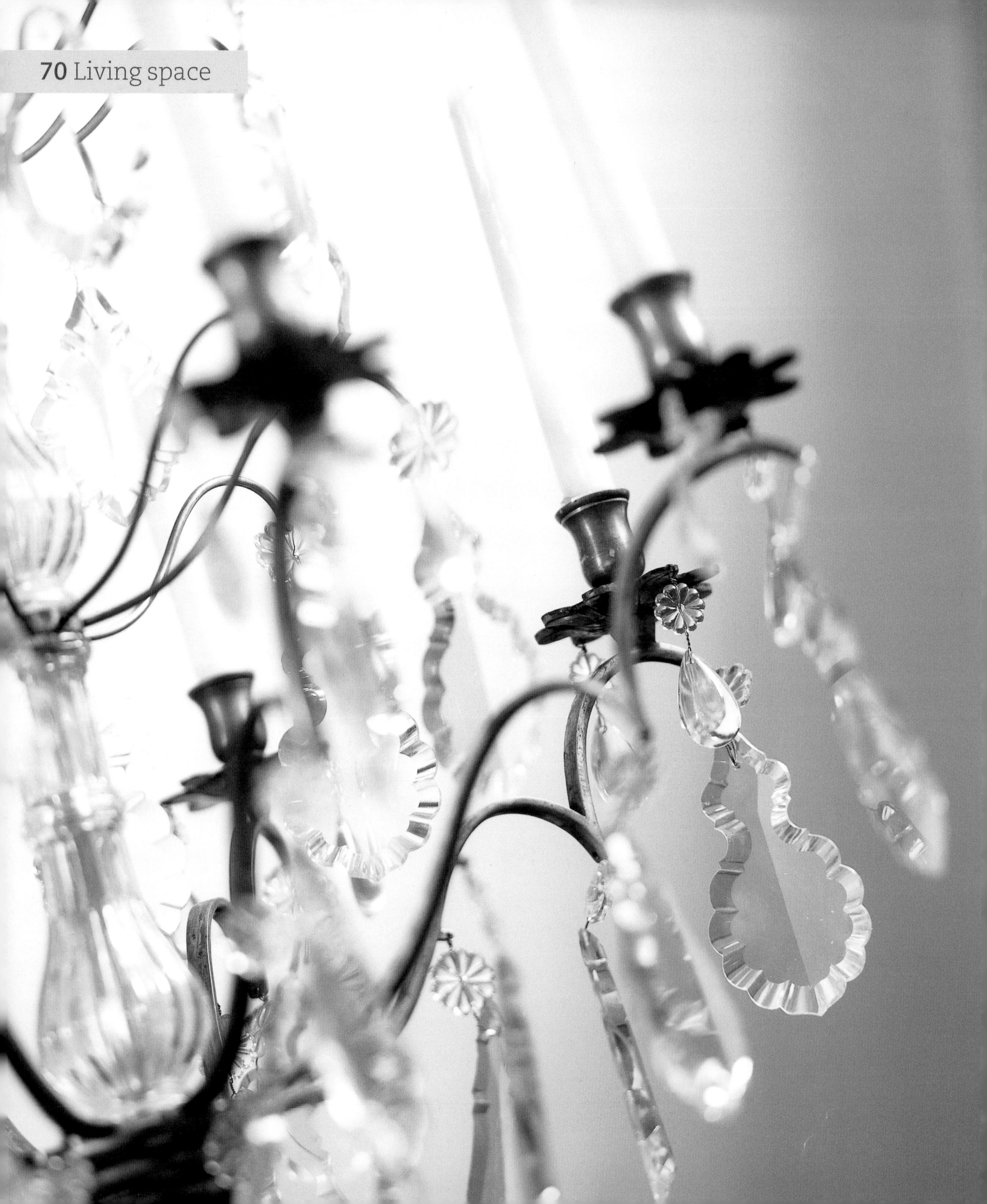

Light

Choosing the right lighting is so important, yet so difficult. Light is what creates atmosphere and brings a living room to life, but it needs to be functional, too. Light for reading, eating, working and relaxing. Light that sparkles, spotlights or accentuates. Soft light that creates a subdued ambience, or gutsy lighting that makes a statement.

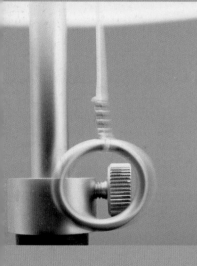

Mood lighting and reading light
When it comes to lighting the various areas of your living room, you need to ask yourself whether you want mood lighting or if you need strong light to read or work by. This sometimes necessitates a variety of fittings with different light intensity, sometimes not: mood lighting and reading light can go very well together, such as the old-fashioned standard lamp or its modern equivalents. Two standard lamps on either side of a sofa, and fitted with 60-watt bulbs, provide adequate light for reading and also create their own ambience. You may not need the same light in the same place all the time. At one time you may be reading the paper, while on another occasion you might be enjoying a drink or a romantic dinner. In that case, you can place different types of lighting together and turn them on or off according to your mood. Dimmers are becoming more and more modish (and also even easier to install by yourself) – a useful innovation which allows you to switch from reading to mood lighting and back again at one simple turn of the hand.

Style
Lamps come in all shapes and sizes – from rustic and nostalgic to austere and modern. Be daring in mixing and matching styles. An old-fashioned lampshade on a stainless-steel lamp stand can create a surprisingly good effect, as can an old wooden lamp stand with a shiny, new lampshade. A row of the same lamps (hanging or standing) looks stylish and harmonious. One extra-large lamp can sometimes look better than three different small ones: play with format. Consider the tone of various lights and choose what suits your interior best: cooler and more sparkling (such as halogen lighting) or warmer and softer (standard light bulbs).

! idea

Lamps can be what set the trends in your interior: a contemporary design in a conspicuous spot can bestow a really up-to-the-minute effect.

Greenery

We can literally bring a room to life by using greenery; interiors become a celebration with the addition of flowers. Plants with distinctive forms in stylish pots are furnishings in themselves. In short, greenery can be a room's finishing touch. Create a plan. Don't leave where you put your greenery to chance. Well-placed plants bring the sun indoors.

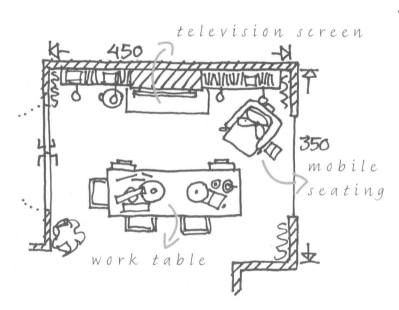

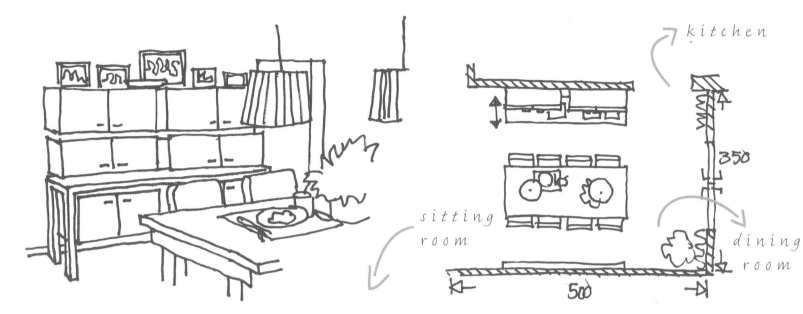

kitchen

sitting room

350

dining room

500

450

television screen

350

mobile seating

work table

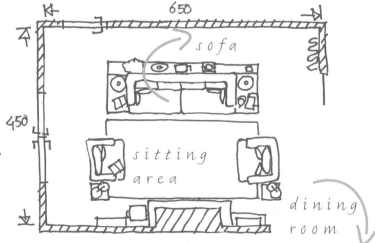

650

sofa

450

sitting area

dining room

Living-space layout

A living room needs a flexible layout. For eating: an extra tabletop running the length of the wall, with cabinets above and below. For working: storage space and shelves on either side of the fireplace, a laptop on the table and a movable armchair in the corner. For sitting in comfort: extended, low shelving units and two end tables enclosing three sides of a large, sprawling sofa.

Chapter 3

Kitchen

This is the heart of the home, where family and friends gather together, where delicious meals are made with care and anticipation. It is a treat for all of the senses, where we might cook up a storm or simply butter a piece of toast.

We all meet up in the kitchen every day: sometimes for a long period of time, sometimes not

Wish list

- layout
- nice floor
- clever details
- organization
- eating
- walls
- light

The kitchen could well merit being called the most efficient room in the house. It is the room we consider most carefully: its layout, practicality and ease of movement, equipment, the materials for the cupboards, work surface and floor, wall coverings, lighting ... A cleverly organized kitchen is one that is pleasant to work in, thereby allowing us to enjoy cooking more – which is why we make all these countless decisions: whether to choose a complete kitchen unit system or to install items separately; whether to have everything set against the wall or to have a cooking island; whether to have open or closed cupboards; whether to suspend cabinets on the wall or stand them on the floor.

But a kitchen is not just about cookery. It is also a place to be lived in. And although we may be focused and concentrating on our tasks in the kitchen, is also the place where we are at our most informal and relaxed in communicating with each other – at the stove together, washing up together, around the kitchen table, talking about the day's events or the most important things in life. Thus the atmosphere in the kitchen is just as important as its efficiency.

What do you want from your kitchen? Ample storage space, new equipment, a large meal table? Is your kitchen at the heart of a lively family or the work place for a busy couple? Do you want rustic-style cosiness or stylish shining chrome – or perhaps both? Your kitchen has to fit in with your lifestyle: make it as beautiful and straightforward as possible for your needs.

idea

The space appointed by the architect for the kitchen does not have to be final. Instead, you should put the kitchen in the place that most suits you; if necessary, use a part of the living room, garage or workshop. Pipes, conduits and cabling can be laid anywhere.

Layout

Important to the style of the kitchen is your **choice of materials.** Bear in mind a kitchen's specific

requirements: materials must be resistant to water and grease. Here, laminate has been used for the walls.

!idea

To make an **open-plan kitchen** look bigger, extend the flooring used in the dining or living room into the kitchen. Place **a second work surface** at the point where the dividing wall used to be.

Culinary ambience: mix work with pleasure

idea

It is easy to make a simple rail for kitchen towels and cloths. To keep them dry between use, place the rail in front of a radiator.

idea

Foodstuffs can be great to look at – the secret is extravagance. A fruit bowl should be filled to the brim, and jars packed with biscuits or cookies.

Layout: the questions to ask

How do you use your kitchen? How much do you like being in the kitchen? Do you use it extensively for cooking, or is the kitchen just somewhere for a quick breakfast or snack? How large is the area that you want to use? The layout of your kitchen depends on your answers to questions such as these. Do you like to ring the changes? If so, a flexible system of separate units is probably better for you than a purpose-built fitted kitchen. Do you like to have contact with family and guests while you are cooking? If so, you might prefer to have a cooking island rather than a unit against a wall, assuming you have the space. Do you need kitchen cupboards above the work surface? Do you want a dish-washer in the kitchen? Or would you rather have several sinks because, for you, washing-up by hand is an essential social moment in your family life?

The floor

A kitchen floor must be able to take a few knocks. Consequently, materials such as linoleum or tiles are well suited. Stone flooring is more expensive, but looks smart and stylish. If your kitchen is open-plan, if possible extend the flooring used in the living room into the kitchen; this creates harmony and unity. Doing this only becomes a problem if carpeting is involved. Wood and even parquet tiling can be specially treated and varnished to make them water-resistant.

Clever details

The kitchen is the ideal place for clever little details. If there is a radiator against a wall, you can incorporate it under the work surface, with grating at the back for aeration, allowing you to have your work surface flush with the wall. And how about a lid in the work surface that conceals a waste bin, allowing you to sweep off any waste into the bin in one easy movement? These ideas require a professional's skill, of course. However, you can put up a simple bar in front of the radiator yourself, and use it for hanging tea towels and cloths: this is a small detail that is easy to add yourself and can make a real difference to your kitchen.

!idea

A luxury kitchen guarantees years of satisfaction. **Do not be afraid to invest.** If your budget is finite, remember that you can make do with just **one kitchen unit,** such as the cooking island shown here.

SURINAAMSE RIJST
LANGE KORREL
RA KWALITEIT

10 KG

Details: elegant sink fittings and roomy display shelves with an articulated lighting system

Roos jarig!

12 nov.

14.00
zwemles

· melk
· eieren
· olijfolie

om
thuis

idea

If you want to adhere to a restrained style of kitchen
(such as seen here: a cooking island with cupboards
in lime-waxed oak and a work surface made of
Belgian bluestone), you should still try to bring in
some element of variety. In a minimalist kitchen,
you could cover a wall with blackboard paint for
shopping lists, drawings and messages.

Organization

If there is one place in a house where it is important to keep things tidy, it is the kitchen. Not only is this hygienic, but also there are so many different things that need their own storage place. And, basically, a kitchen looks so much better and more appealing if it's not a mess. A tidy kitchen also means less stress for you when cooking.

i!dea Should you store things neatly on open shelving or in cupboards? Try combining both: **open to view**

A tidy kitchen means an uncluttered home and an uncluttered head

and accessible on the 'working side'; everything on the other side stored behind closed doors.

Tidiness behind closed doors

Nobody wants their kitchen to look like a series of supermarket shelves. You can conceal all of your packages, packets, cans, jars, knives and forks, bowls and dishes, cookware and utensils behind cupboard doors. Behind the doors, everything is well organized. There are legions of clever systems on sale that ensure you never again pop things into deep kitchen cabinets at random – and are never quite able to reach whatever is hidden behind. If possible, choose kitchen units with deep drawers that can be pulled out fully, allowing you complete access. A pull-out cupboard with shelves as seen on the left is ideal. A display cabinet or old kitchen dresser with glass doors is useful for tableware that you want to put on show.

Tidiness: small kitchens

Keeping things tidy in a small kitchen means being creative with the space that you have. Cupboards with sliding doors give you more room to move and can also be used as notice boards. If you have very little floor space, make sure you use all of the vertical space instead. A double row of kitchen cabinets, or a cupboard that reaches to the ceiling with its own ladder for access to the topmost shelves, will provide you with an abundance of storage space. Doors give a small kitchen a orderly yet uncramped look.

Tidiness with everything on view

Shelves or open-shelving units look informal and cheerful. They are an alternative to cupboards that you can make yourself from planks of wood or MDF. Dinnerware and attractively packaged foods can be used as decoration for the kitchen. In addition to kitchen pans, you can hang up anything, from strings of chilli peppers to drawings, using clips on a suspended rod. Smaller items could be grouped together in attractive boxes or baskets.

Eating

Eating in the kitchen is different to eating in the dining room. The bustling cheeriness makes your kitchen the most informal place in the house. Pulling up to the kitchen table encourages a cosy, relaxed feeling. Whether talking with friends long into the night or grabbing a hurried breakfast early in the morning, eating in the kitchen is always a pleasure.

Seating in every kitchen

Even in the smallest kitchen, some corner can be found where a shelf or foldaway table will fit along a wall: above a radiator or in front of a window, with a wide window-seat doubling as a tabletop; in a corner, or between the refrigerator and a tall cupboard. Paint the wall behind the table with blackboard paint or else hang up a notice board. Just as with the hall, this is a central meeting point which everyone passes. If your kitchen is roomy enough, choose a large table that everyone can sit round – although a surprising number of people will fit at even a small table, as long as the kitchen is welcoming. It is a good idea for kitchen tables to be quite robust to allow for spills and scratches.

! idea

A small, simple surface is quite enough to create a quick breakfast area: here, a wide shelf has been fixed to a wall covered in cheerful pink blackboard paint.

maandag
zwemles

Walls

Kitchen walls never stand empty. They carry cupboards full of vital items, and racks of kitchen utensils. They arm themselves against grease and condensation with coverings of wood, plastic, metal or tiles. They are made for you to attach recipes, notes and shopping lists. A kitchen's walls have their work cut out.

! idea

The design of this kitchen has been kept restrained, and its quality can be seen in the different materials used throughout: a Spanish limestone floor, a Portuguese bluestone work surface, oak cupboards. A mixture of materials has also been used for the walls: wide, suspended shelves, plaster and, behind the stove, handmade Spanish tiling.

A varied view: tiles where they are necessary and plasterwork wherever possible

What should go on the wall?

A kitchen wall has many functions and therefore needs to be strong and practical. Plasterwork is fine in principle, but a wipe-clean wall above a work surface or stove is far more practical. To achieve this you could finish your wall with metalwork, varnished wood panelling, tiles, or perhaps a special paint – it all depends on your style and budget. A great deal can be stored hung from hooks on horizontal bars fixed to the wall. Attach white suspended shelves to a dark background and create a distinctive, open storage space. Do not be afraid to combine different materials: plasterwork, tiles, wood, for example.

Light

Kitchen lighting is often task lighting. Make sure you have good light to work by above the work surfaces and stove. This can be achieved with simple spotlights in the ceiling, but you might also consider using 'ordinary' table lamps or even adjustable standard lamps: these make the kitchen feel homier and warmer (see photograph on page 108). Spots can be incorporated within thick suspended shelves as well – as can additional sockets. Industrial ceiling lamps above a work surface look attractive and are useful, too. Another idea is to employ task lighting above the work space while creating mood lighting in some other part of the kitchen; this enhances the kitchen beyond the level of just a work place.

Kitchen walls
do not have to be
merely practical;
there is nothing
wrong with
having fun, too,
with photographs
and pictures

idea

Vary the lighting used in the kitchen. Spotlights can be built into the underside of shelving if it is thick enough; industrial ceiling lamps look impressive over a central island; table lamps are unexpected on a work surface but create a homey feel.

Lighting: subdued or crisp; practical or elegant?

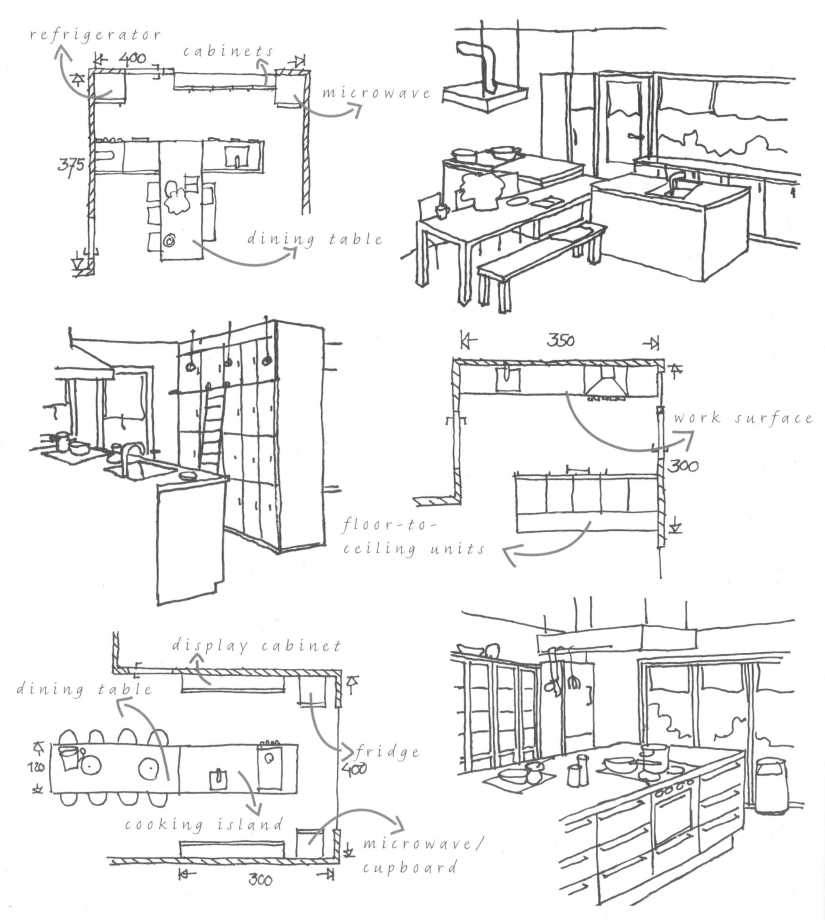

refrigerator

400

cabinets

microwave

375

dining table

work surface

350

300

floor-to-ceiling units

display cabinet

dining table

120

fridge

400

cooking island

microwave/ cupboard

300

Kitchen layout

Kitchens are open to many layout interpretations. You could 'close off' an open-plan kitchen by placing two tall storage units back to back: kitchen utensils on the kitchen side, books on the living-room side. Cooking and eating give you a central place to set a dining table between two work-surface areas. What's more, you can create an extra dining area and work surface by placing a large table at one end of a cooking island.

Chapter 4

Bedroom

A room to sleep in, then wake refreshed. A room for warmth and tranquillity, relaxation and indulgence, love and languidness, tenderness and calm – even for work and exercise. The bedroom is our personal oasis in a hectic world.

A personal space in which to unwind with an ambience that reflects who you are

Wish list

- *relaxation*
- *activity*
- *organization*
- *walls and floors*
- *attractive fabrics*

The time has long since past when we hastily pulled the covers over our heads at night and sped from the bedroom in the morning shivering with cold. Today we want to have as many options open to us in the bedroom as we do in the living room. This means that the bedroom is not merely for sleeping in, but also for living in: for relaxation, breakfasting, browsing the Internet, reading, watching television, listening to music or working in earnest. The bedroom is no longer the poor relation in the house, but constitutes an integral part of its interior. Nonetheless, the bedroom remains unique. The living room belongs to everyone. The bedroom is private: a space in which to unwind, to be alone, where you can snuggle up without prying eyes – in short, a comfortable place in which to retreat from the world.

To create an environment in the bedroom that makes us feel happy and enables us to do everything as we want takes more than simply choosing a bed and a wardrobe. We need adequate storage facilities and an ingenious layout so that there is somewhere to put all our clothes, shoes, books, furniture, equipment and whatever else we want to have around us. Otherwise we cannot create the tranquillity and space we need to breathe and live. Next, we personalize the room and make it more appealing using the colours, materials and objects that we love most.

! idea

Re-create the ambience of your living room to create a fully-fledged bedroom interior. Allow the subtle reappearance of colours, textiles and furnishings. The bed and other usual bedroom furniture already do enough to give this room its distinctive character, so the spaces won't feel the same but will have a coherence.

!idea

Choose the room you feel **most comfortable** in to be your bedroom. Do you want it dark or well lit; large or small? Once you have decided on location, put your bed in the part of the room you like best. Create a relaxed living **space with warm blankets** and a television (or not, if that is not your idea of relaxation).

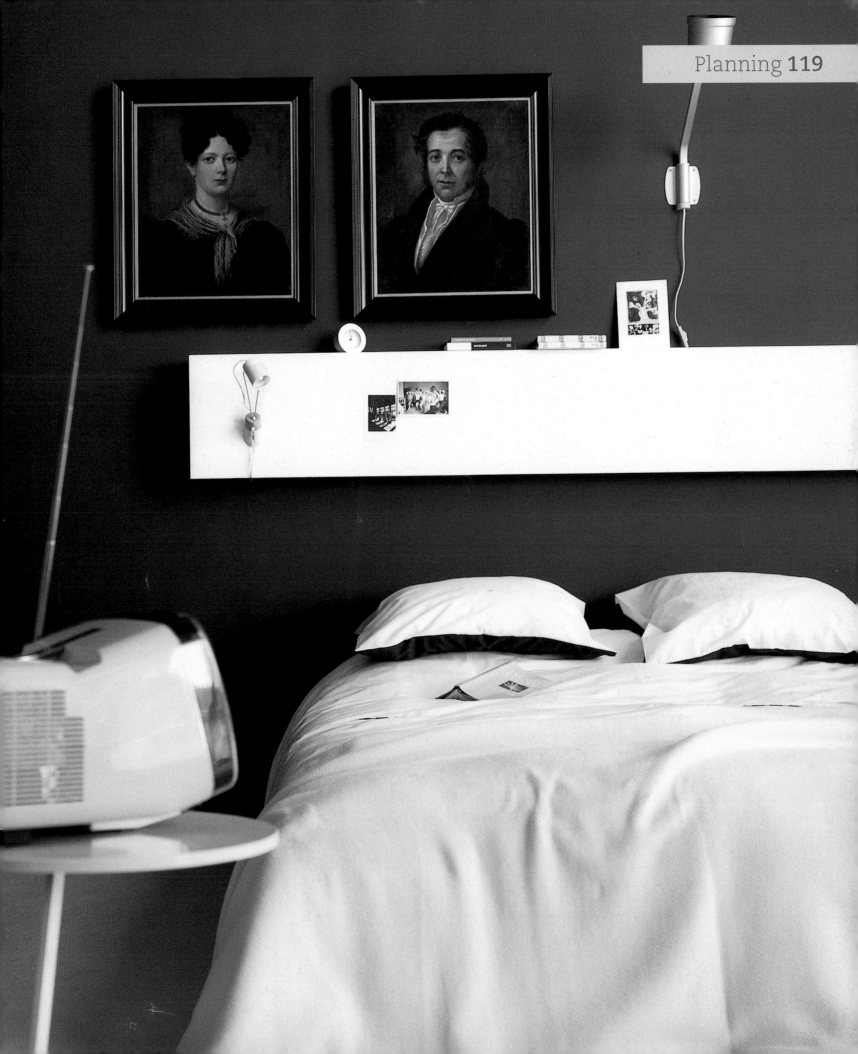

Relaxation

The bedroom is the most personal room in the house. It is where we want to relax and indulge our senses. That is why it is a room replete with comfortable materials and beautiful things. Often, we have a tendency to fill our bedrooms with second-rate clutter, which certainly does no justice to the room's potential. Turn this room into a place where you can relax by using lots of soft throws, blankets and cushions or pillows. Use colours that are cheery and uplifting. Fill it with things that are precious to you and that you love to look at. Hang artwork on the walls, have candles or vases of flowers. Turn this space into the most personalized living space possible.

Activity

The bedroom can also be an excellent space for working, breakfasting, exercising and so on. A low table or a bench placed at the foot of the bed gives you space for a television, books and also an additional seating area. A higher table on casters, if wide enough to be rolled over the bed, allows you to work or breakfast under the bedcovers. An ordinary table can be used as a writing desk, as a dressing table or as a breakfast table. And have you ever considered putting your books in the bedroom instead of the living room, with a roomy armchair right next to them?

A bed is not only a place for sleeping, but also a place to sit. A fabulous oversized sofa.

Organization

There are so many things to cram into the bedroom. Clothes and shoes, blankets and bed linen, books and magazines, a clock and radio ... We do far more than just sleep in our bedroom and we don't always have our eyes shut in there. Above all, create a restful atmosphere – a tidy bedroom gives space in which to breathe.

Organized layout A bedroom needs breathing space and room enough to walk around without bumping into the furniture. That is why it is important to be as ingenious as possible about arranging your space. Is your bedroom large enough? If it is, why not consider converting part of it into a walk-in closet, perhaps with sliding doors. It does not have to be the size of a dancehall, but it will give you an exceptional feeling of luxury to have your clothing so well organized. Another way to separate the storage side of your room is to construct a (sliding) partition behind the head of your bed. Behind it, you can store dressers or a clothes rack and shelving. Try to be more unorthodox in the way you think about the layout of your bedroom – it should be about what makes you comfortable. Would a large four-poster bed in the middle of the room make you happy? Then go ahead and get one. Do you have a fireplace? Then put a fleece rug in front of it, plus a comfy armchair, or move the end of the bed towards the fire. Do you work a lot in your bedroom? Then put your writing desk in the best spot.

Storage Cupboards and wardrobes are essential for storing everything that we want to keep out of sight in the bedroom. Apart from the much-prized walk-in closet, the most orderly effect is gained by using wardrobes, drawers and storage units with doors: an unbelievable amount can be stored inside. A wall unit avoids the impression of a room filled with large pieces of furniture. Mirrors on the doors will make the room lighter and also appear larger. Alternatively, you might have an antique dresser or some other treasured piece of furniture. Simple storage units can be made more special if you place several together, decorating their doors identically. One or more shelves above the bed take up less space than bedside tables. And, just as in the living room, everything that you love to look at may be in full view – special objects in an open cupboard and personal photographs on the wall.

idea

Hanging and storage space can be concealed behind a movable screen placed at the head of the bed. If there is no room for this, choose attractive wardrobes, armoires or other storage units instead. Position two identical examples side by side, perhaps, for a his-and-hers effect.

!idea

Make sure there is a mixture of designs on the bed. Buy **separate pillowcases** with every duvet cover. Only use cotton bedding: it has a **crisp, fresh look.**

Walls Be daring with colour because colour adds to your bedroom's ambience. One red wall at the head of the bed creates warmth and intimacy. Red and shades of red make a room warm and cheerful; blues and pastels are refreshing and create calm as well as an illusion of depth. Yellow makes a bedroom sunny. Do not forget the ceiling. After all, you notice it here more than in any other room. A sky-blue painted ceiling gives you the sense that you are out in the open looking up above.

Floor The bedroom should be a place to indulge all our senses, including – if not especially – the sense of touch. It is a place where you must be able to walk barefoot. Thus the bedroom floor should feel soft and warm, and that could even mean a hard floor with woolly rugs. A bedroom floor has less traffic on it than a living-room floor, so softer and less hardwearing carpeting is an option.

Attractive fabrics Curtains, drapes, throws, rugs, cushions, pillows and sheets lend colour and style to the bedroom. If you do not want to paint your walls in bright colours straightaway, use colour in fabrics. Be as extravagant as you want with cushions and pillows: they provide a sumptuous sense of luxury, and you can use them for resting your head, supporting your back, sitting on or simply looking at. The more cushions, pillows, rugs and throws you use (either in bright colours jumbled together or in tones of just one hue), the greater the impression you will make.

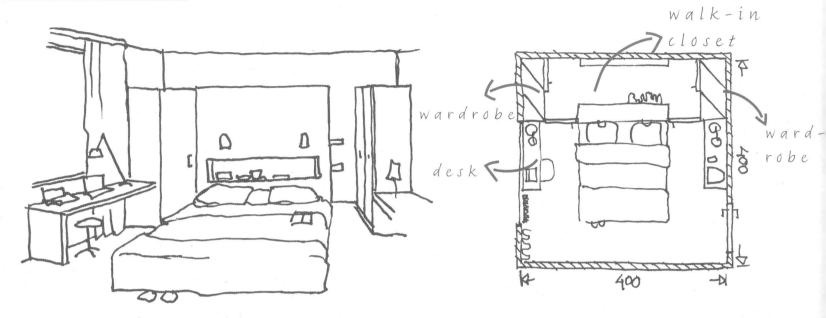

walk-in closet

wardrobe

ward-robe

desk

400

400

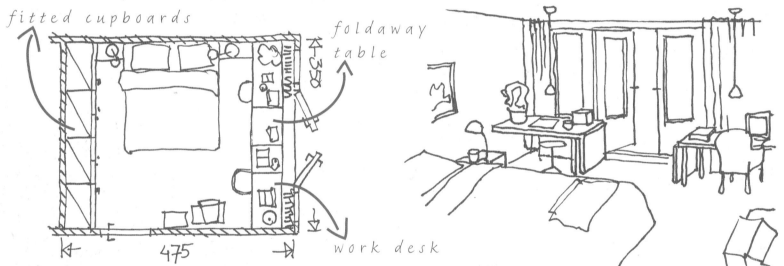

fitted cupboards

foldaway table

350

work desk

475

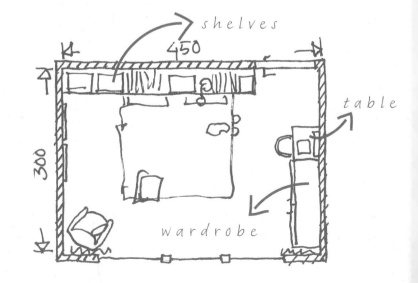

shelves

table

450

300

wardrobe

Bedroom layout

Put your bedroom to full use. Build a walk-in wardrobe or closet by erecting a partition wall at the head of the bed: you can hang and store clothing on one side, while on the other you can make a niche for your alarm clock. In front of the double doors you can create a flexible work area with foldaway table leaves. Or else, put up shelving around the bed from wall to wall.

Chapter 5

Bathroom

A place for a hasty wash or for lazy relaxation, whether at the beginning of the day or at its end. It's where we pep up in a hurry, play, or pamper ourselves. Ultimately, the bathroom is where body and soul are cleansed and revived.

Enjoy the luxury
of a warm bath
in complete
tranquillity

Wish list

- *luxury*
- *style*
- *organization*
- *family bathroom*
- *layout*
- *clever details*
- *materials*

The days are gone when each morning we leapt, shivering, into the shower, and the bathroom was little more than a cell in which to keep clean. Nowadays we use the bathroom not only for showering and bathing, but also for relaxation and fun; we use it to unwind and to play in. As a result, the bathroom has an increased role in our lives and thus it is important that we feel comfortable when using it.

To create an ambience, the same rule applies as in the rest of the house: bring your personal taste to life. What is your favourite style – opulent or minimalist? Or, perhaps, both opulent and minimalist? Do you love indulging yourself in the plush luxury of a hotel bathroom? Or are you more attracted to the austere simplicity of a purely functional bathroom? What are your favourite materials?

Each bathroom is different, of course, and every household is different as well. What kind of space do you want your bathroom to be? Is yours a family bathroom where everyone has to fight for their space during the 'rush hour'? Or do you want it, above all, to be a calming space in which to retreat? Let your circumstances determine the bathroom's design; the right ambience will then evolve by itself.

An elegant feel can be created by maintaining the simplicity of the room with appropriate storage. True luxury involves the use of costly materials, of course, but even so, a simple bathroom can appear luxurious if thought is given to its layout and ingenuity figures in its details.

! idea

Don't cram too much into a bathroom. The golden rule really is 'less is more'. Keep its essentials simple. Introduce only one or two main colours, preferably as neutral as possible. Let accessories be responsible for providing any colour accents.

!idea

Use **durable materials**, to attain a sense of timeless luxury: polished wood surfaces, glass and moulded flooring. These are well worth investing in. Think about practicality as well: sink units incorporating drawers and **wide towel rails** demonstrate a good use of space.

Luxury

A bathroom's luxury is evident in the overall picture – in its straight lines and gleaming surfaces, and in its generous proportions. It is in the natural materials used to create a warm effect and in its serene, ordered appearance. Luxury is also in the details: simple but high-quality accessories; thick, extra-soft towels; ingenious storage. After all, this is where we care for and pamper ourselves.

Style How do you achieve a luxurious effect in the bathroom? Luxury is found principally in expensive fixtures and fittings, such as elegant materials, a power-shower, a whirlpool bath or steam sauna cabin, and many more such novelties besides. Yet however wonderful all these extras may be, they are not the be-all and end-all. Luxury can be achieved without a sauna. It is all about a feeling for style. Achieve a contemporary feeling of luxury by mixing styles: an exciting combination of wood and metal, basic tones mixed with a brightly coloured accent, frivolous elements within a sober design scheme. Adapt the old to a new situation: paint an old cupboard; raise a low free-standing bathtub onto sturdy blocks or mount it on a platform in the same material as the floor or in the same colour as the walls.

Organization A bathroom is a place of purity and freshness; this space has to make a clean impression. Store as much as possible out of sight behind doors and in drawers. Wall-mounted suspended sinks work well in providing more space. Drawers set below – perhaps with towel rails attached to them – give you space for all your things. If they are an option, wall niches are a great solution for bottles and items that need to be on hand when showering. Cast a critical eye over your assembled pots, jars and bottles; throw away anything that is ugly or never used. Buy a set of glass bottles or separate boxes for your smaller items to create a tidy, elegant-looking bathroom at a stroke.

The satisfaction a bathroom gives lies in the details, so pay attention to taps (faucets) and showerheads.

idea

If you have children, choose a grown-up underlying style and adjust the details and accessories to suit the children's ages. Those elephant-trunk towel hooks can always be replaced later by more sophisticated ones – and children grow up before you know it.

Family bathroom

Above all when you have children in the home, the bathroom has to be clean and practical. And there should be a bit of fun about it, too, as it helps a great deal if children enjoy bathtime. A walk-in shower, two taps (faucets) above a well-proportioned sink, an additional shower attachment in the bath if several children have to be bathed at once or as an aid to hair-washing, and lots of hooks to keep everything off the floor – all are useful details to include. One clever idea (see below left) is to use a CD rack with a Perspex front, set horizontally, to hold all manner of bathroom clutter.

Room for everyone to bathe,

shower or splash about

!idea

If you have a large bathroom, you may decide to conceal the sink or shower cubicle behind a partition wall. If your bathroom is extremely small, on the other hand, consider knocking through to an adjacent room to enlarge it.

! idea

Quick and efficient for the whole family: a washing area with a double shower and a partition wall with a sink.

Layout

It is worth considering devoting more space to the bathroom if you can: by incorporating a small adjoining room within it or by converting another, larger room into your bathroom instead of using the existing one. If you have no renovation plans at present, there is still a lot to be gained from having a good layout. Bathroom fixtures can be obtained in many sizes nowadays, and there is no need to be overly conservative and keep them all ranged against a wall. Something that works wonderfully, even in a smaller room, is to have a full- or half-length partition wall. You can then install the shower on one side and the sink(s) on the other – attractive, contemporary and efficient.

Clever details

Being a functional space, the bathroom is the place to employ practical details. For example, consider long rails or hooks on which to hang facecloths and towels, or other things that have to be kept off the floor. Rails serve well set against a wall, in front of a radiator or as handles on drawers. Think laterally: a rack intended for CDs, stationery items or herbs and spices can be ideal as a container for moisturizers and shampoo bottles. A strong box on casters can serve as a laundry hamper, stool and occasional table all in one.

Materials

When we think of bathrooms we almost automatically think of tiles, which can be obtained in every variety, shape and size. Try experimenting with tiles of the same colour but in different sizes. Almost all materials can now be used in the bathroom without difficulty. Stainless steel is functional and looks smart and contemporary. Wood is luxurious and exudes warmth. A moulded floor is minimalist and easy to clean. Find out what your options are: the possibilities are endless.

Laundry

If you are combining the laundry room with the bathroom, set out a separate area for this function. Use every bit of space. Consider having your clothes-washing area behind a shoulder-height partition or behind doors. Stack machines on top of each other. Keep colours to a minimum, and coordinate with those in the bathroom. If necessary, you can even custom-build your own piece of furniture to conceal it.

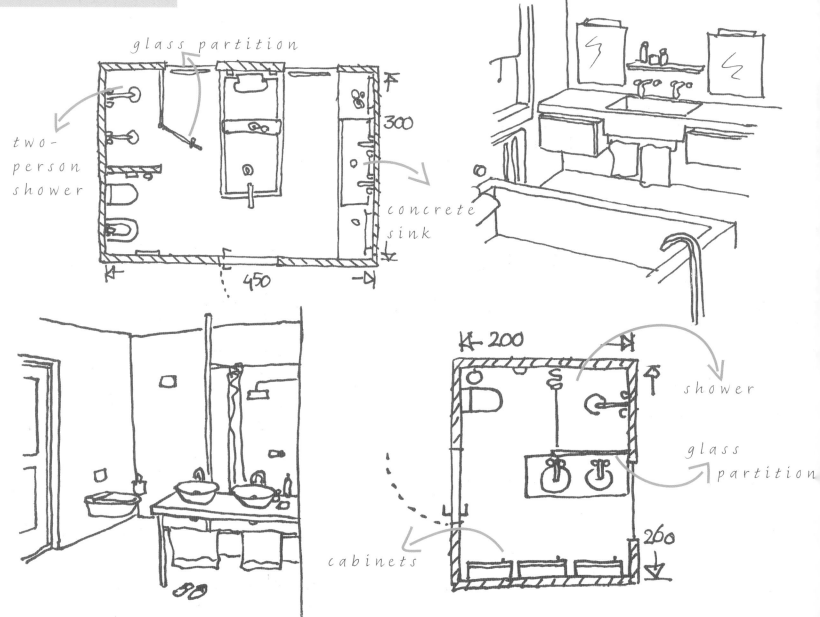

glass partition

two-person shower

concrete sink

300

450

shower

glass partition

cabinets

200

260

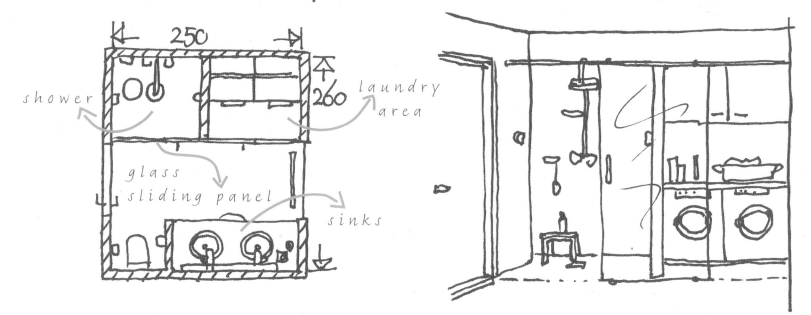

shower

glass sliding panel

laundry area

sinks

250

260

Bathroom layout

Good layout makes a bathroom efficient and beautiful. You can custom-build the room's basic structure in concrete, including the bathtub, washstand/sink, a two-person shower and a bidet. A frosted-glass partition with a shower on one side and the sinks on the other creates an open feeling. And a glass sliding partition neatly separates the washing machine/clothes drier from the shower.

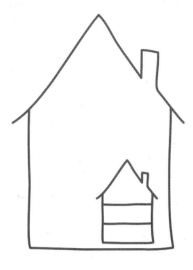

Chapter 6

Children

A nest for a baby. A place to play and romp about in. Somewhere to do homework and chill with friends … A child's room is their own little world where they can build castles in the air, express themselves freely and discover who they are.

*A child's room:
just that little
bit more creative,
that little bit
more adventurous*

Wish list:

- from baby to toddler
- older children
- their own colours, own style
- their own domain
- solutions for smaller rooms
- organization

A child will often have the same room for years, so the space needs to be able to change and evolve with the progression of childhood. The baby's room is a safe, quiet nest of your own creation. The older your child becomes, the more the cosy baby's room changes into your child's own domain, filled with their own belongings, with things made at school, with girls' things or boys' things. From a storage space for toddlers' toys it gradually – though sooner than you think – becomes a hiding place and playroom for growing children. Finally, it changes from a playroom to a study, a teenager's room where the door is closed, music thuds out and idols adorn the walls.

Older children have their own opinions about how their rooms should be decorated. And can you blame them? It is the only room in the house to which they can retreat. This chapter is filled with ideas to help you and your child choose a personal colour and style. It also offers solutions for the room that seems just that bit too small and ensures that keeping it tidy ceases to be a chore.

idea

Combine robust elements with gentle details in a baby's room. This provides an interesting contrast. If you keep the colours neutral, it is easier to turn it into a toddler's room (or a room for your next baby).

!idea

It is fine to let a child's room be quite different from the rest of the house in terms of the style and feel of its interior. Think more along the lines of playfulness and nonchalance. Children love being in surroundings that are designed especially for them.

From baby to toddler

A baby's room does not have to be sugary sweet – you soon tire of it and, what's more, your child soon grows out of it. Instead, give it a more robust interpretation, but with a nod to childhood – such as a neutral white and dove-grey colour scheme, with soft touches or quirky details. Consider buying flexible, multifunctional furniture which can be used in different ways as needs change. If the baby's room is also to be a child's room, make sure there is enough room for play. Have one large wardrobe instead of numerous smaller pieces of furniture, and put a soft rug on the floor. Arrange 'treasures' and homemade things on shelves and in cabinets on the wall, as shown in the photograph below right.

Op 13 juni
wordt
Mette
8 jaar

!idea

For as long as it remains possible to banish Top 10 posters from covering the walls of the room, turn the children's room into a museum-in-miniature using 'treasure boxes'. If necessary, give your children picture frames to display music and football heroes.

Older children

All of a sudden, your children develop their own sense of self. Suddenly, the things they have are 'stupid' and what they want to have is 'cool'. Suddenly, a desk appears, then mysterious books and papers ... locks on the drawers ... locks on the door. Time for their own opinions. Their own style. Their own decisions. Still, a little nudge in the right direction can't hurt ...

Their own colours and style

As children grow older, they become better able to express themselves and their own opinions. They want to be involved in making decisions about how their rooms should look. How best to guide them with this and how can you let them go their own way without sinking into despair at their dubious sense of taste and childish kitsch? A Bob-the-Builder paradise might seem a good idea to a child, but it is likely to grate with you in no time. Start off with ideas about colour and paint. Let them choose their own colours, either freely or else giving them ten options from which to choose. You can then use the favourite colour(s) in the furniture, walls and bed linen. Remember, painting one wall or stripe will be enough when using a bright colour. Let them think up a creative idea of their own: stripes or dots on the wall, or a number or letter above the bed. One idea for a rainy afternoon is to get them to cut out pictures from interior design and home decoration magazines to help them choose the styles and colours they like most. The inevitable – and not always so very attractive – posters and collections can be framed or housed in cupboards chosen by you.

Their own domain

Sometimes two children have to share the same room: sleeping, playing and learning in one space. You could consider a number of options to stop them being at each other's throats. The first of these is to give each child his or her own 'domain', with his or her own cupboards, hooks, baskets and colour scheme. A division in the form of a low or high chest of drawers is easy to put in place. A more drastic option is to place within the bedroom a well-ventilated, mobile 'box room' made from MDF or wood, with space for a bed and desk (see photograph opposite, below right).

idea

Don't crowd too many things into a child's room. It makes tidying up that much easier on the child. An overcrowded room that gets into a shambles is just a dreadful chore.

idea

Children are creative and uninhibited. Let them surprise you with their ideas. Sometimes a child's room will produce such exciting results that you will be asking for their advice on the living room.

idea

Space savers: a multifunctional
work surface placed either side of the chimney
breast and along the whole length of the room,
with the **bed placed above.**

Sleeping in the clouds; learning on the ground floor

Solutions for smaller rooms
A small room sometimes has more solutions on offer than you might think at first sight. Put as much as possible of the available space to good use. For example, rather than having a separate, free-standing desk, install a custom-made work surface running along the length of one wall. Put lots of drawers underneath. Use the room's full height: cupboards to the ceiling or a bed on a raised platform – this is a tried-and-tested space saver with enough room below for toys, an additional bed, or a desk.

Organization
How are you to keep your children's toys, creations and personal mess tidy? How to keep a check on the mountains of clutter that seem to flow unceasingly into the house? There are several ideas you can use to tackle this problem, depending on your taste and style. For example, boxes, baskets and hooks: make sure there are plenty of these solutions to hand, and label them. Paint cupboard doors in blackboard paint: you can write on them to indicate contents, and there will be room for additional drawing. A basket you can hoist up on a rope from a pulley on the ceiling is ideal for storing toys. Crates on wheels under the bed can be used for all sorts of things. Think about baskets for dirty clothes, as a big toy box, or for a waste bin – perhaps on wheels – and have separate cupboards and shelves for all those bits and pieces that accumulate as your child gets older.

idea

A **movable screen** between the sleeping and studying areas brings a little more order to both and, moreover, offers flexibility when it comes to the **changing needs** of a teenage daughter and her critical girlfriends.

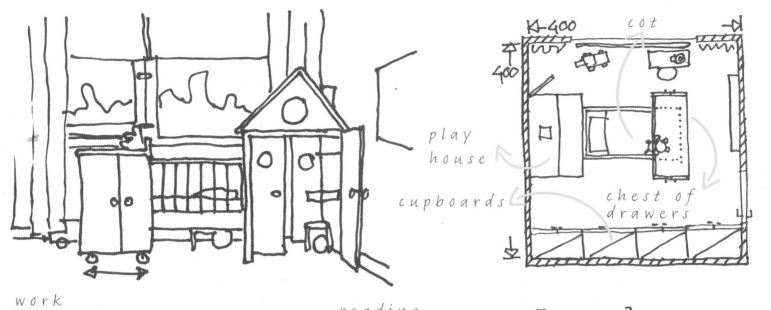

play
house

cupboards

←─ 400

400

cot

chest of
drawers

work
desk

reading
desk

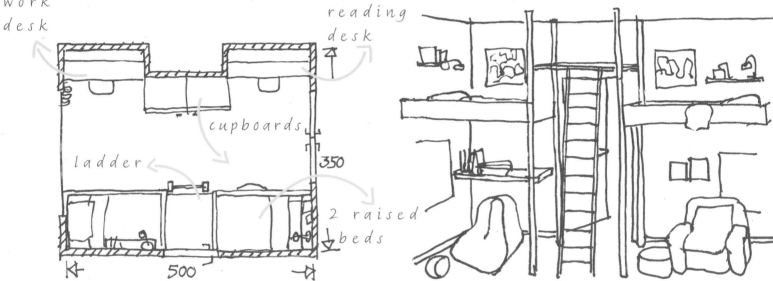

cupboards

ladder

350

2 raised
beds

←─── 500 ─→

desk

cupboards

550

bed

open
shelvin

←── 450 ─→

Children's layout

You can create a baby's or toddler's room, leaving options open for when they grow older, by putting a play house at the head of the bed and a (movable) chest of drawers or cupboard at the end, mounted with a tabletop. Two raised beds either side of the door save space on the floor below for sitting and playing in. Children who share a room retain their own space if you build a cruciform partition to give each one an area for a bed and desk.

Chapter 7

Work space

On the sofa with a notepad, at the kitchen table with your laptop, at a desk that folds away into a cupboard when not in use, or in a fully equipped study ... The where does not matter as long as your surroundings are pleasant to work in.

An office space
at home in your
own style: it
makes working
that bit better!

Wish list

- *screened off / not screened off*
- *permanent / temporary*
- *organization*
- *working in style*
- *spare room / study*
- *light*

You can choose to work in a separate room set aside specifically for this purpose, but you can also work successfully in numerous other places in the home. We can work wherever there is space, even if we just squeeze in temporarily. The living room, for example. We love to use it for relaxation, but all the same we want – or need – to be able to work there sometimes. Working in the living room can be quite fun. When designing the layout, decide how much you want to screen yourself off from other people. What do you prefer? To be integral to the life of your home, or to cocoon yourself away from everyone?

Work corners can be put anywhere in whatever style you want. The only essential advice is to make it feel homey and not like being at the office. If your work space has panache, you will feel happier about completing your tasks. See whether you have room for a permanent work space (there usually is somewhere; under the stairs or in the spare room, for example), or adopt a flexible, temporary area – one that hides you from view if you so wish. Incorporate useful storage systems in the best way to order your specific business and arrange lighting that goes beyond the obligatory desk lamp.

idea

An ideal flexible work space: everything on wheels, a portable telephone and a laptop. You can set to work wherever you want, just how you like and wherever there is room – even in the garden if the sun is shining.

idea Should you be screened off or not? An MDF partition is used to **separate the desk from the rest** of the room, creating an **intimate work space**, but not isolating you from home life.

idea
Here, instead of an armchair in front of the bookcase, there is an additional desk. Use a laptop for this work space: computers (even designer ones) look ugly from behind with their tangle of cables and wires.

idea

A multifunctional work space in a small house. Each person has a table of his or her own, and these can be joined together for the evening meal. The combination of different types of wood creates a sophisticated effect.

Screened off / not screened off

One person may want to remain part of whatever else is going on in a room while working in it; another may seek out a place that provides a little sanctuary of privacy and quiet. for the latter you will have to reserve a private spot in the room and screen it off using a partition wall or (wooden) screen. This effect can also be achieved using a full bookcase set at right angles to a wall. A homemade, and ingeniously sheltered, work station which incorporates hinges on the wall and wheels attached to it underneath can be seen in the small photograph (right). The entire work space can be turned to the wall in one motion. If you do not need to screen yourself off, get yourself an extra-large dining table on which to put your laptop computer. A comfortable office chair can be squeezed easily between any other chairs you have around it.

Permanent / temporary

Ask yourself how often you want to work in the living room and whether your paperwork can be left where it is. If not, you need a portable office. But if you can do so, select a permanent spot, such as a separate table. Choose your 'office furniture' carefully. Cheap or overly businesslike office furniture looks out of place in a living room; consider less orthodox solutions – something that corresponds with the style, colours and materials employed in your interior. Get a table like the dining table, but use it as a desk, or an antique desk and a shelving unit for papers. Use a flatscreen monitor or a laptop to avoid the hulking mass of a regular computer.

Organization

Working at home often means a lot of mess. Store as much as possible behind doors and in drawers. You can get cabinets that will contain an entire desk and computer behind its doors. Chests of drawers or sideboards are perfect storage options for papers, folders and files, and they certainly look a lot better than standard office cabinets. Baskets, boxes or crates can be put to excellent use as archives.

Orderly, practical, light
and personalized: the
ideal space for working

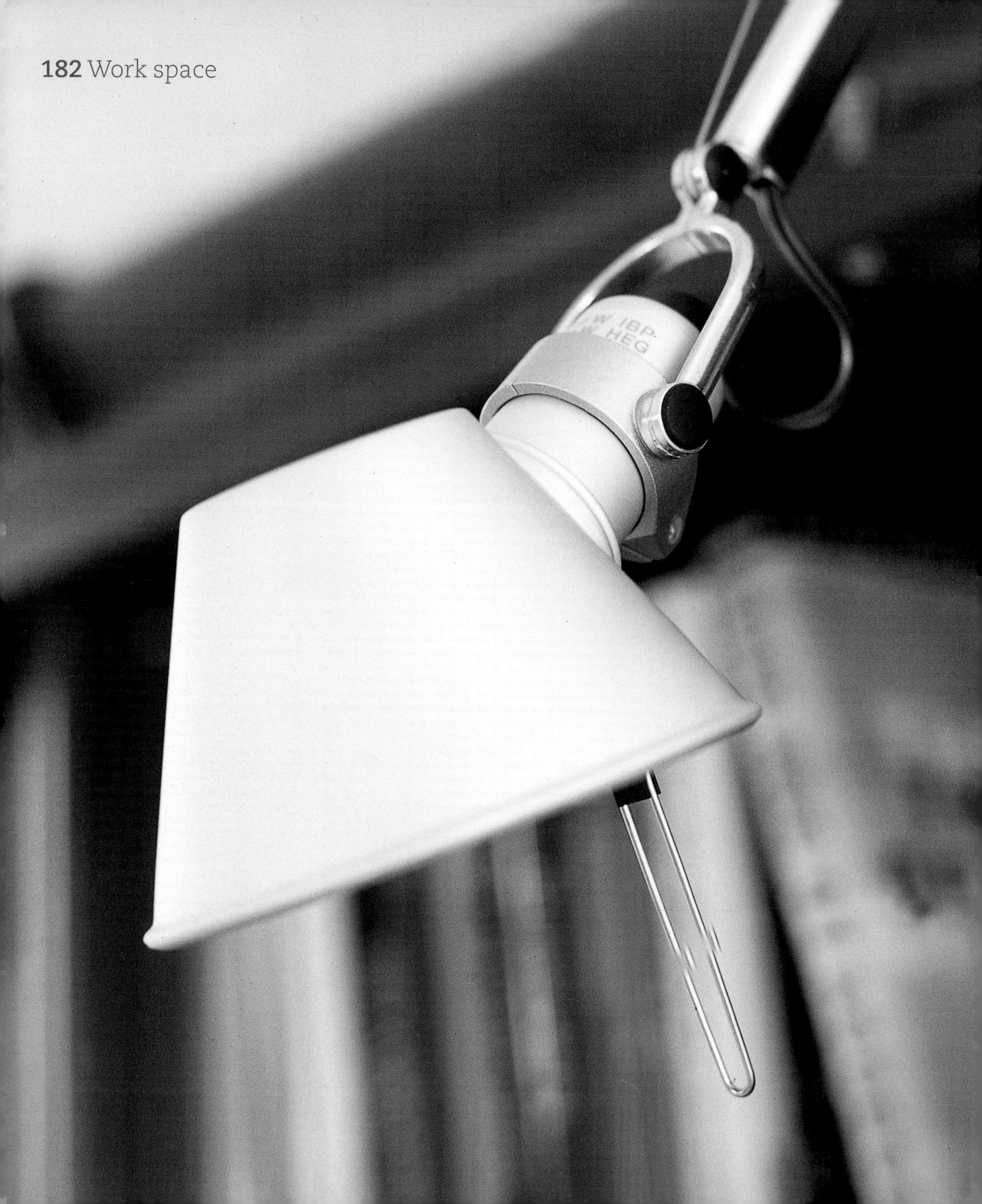

Working in style
When arranging your work place, instead of setting out to create an efficient 'regular' office style, adopt your own style – and the same holds true if your clients visit you regularly (perhaps with all the more reason). After all, this is one of the advantages of working from home: it is not supposed to be some antiseptic space where the air-conditioning hums, but a homely place where the fire crackles. Encourage inspiration by surrounding yourself with beautiful things. Choose a design that coincides with your favourite colours and materials. Store papers in identical labelled crates. Buy metal boxes in which to keep pens and paperclips. Put up a corkboard or blackboard above your desk. Lean a ladder or foldaway steps against a high bookcase containing files and folders.

Spare room / study
Not everyone has the luxury of a separate room devoted exclusively to office use. However, you might well be able to create a combined spare room and study. It is important to achieve the right balance when doing this: make sure that neither of the room's dual functions dominates. All things considered, you will not enjoy always working in what is a 'spare room' (something rather more professional would be better), and it is equally not the most considerate thing to house your guests in the 'office'. The keyword is inspiration. Allow yourself and your guests to benefit from your best ideas. And tidy up properly.

Light
It is essential to have both directional and mood lighting above a desk. Remember not to allow it seem too office-like here either: a table lamp or standard lamp gives out a lot of light and looks attractive. Nor should chandeliers or candlesticks be dismissed out of hand. They can provide your work space with a cheering glow as a complement to a bright desk lamp.

mobile screen
`in front of
work space

KF 400

400

shelves

deep
cupboards

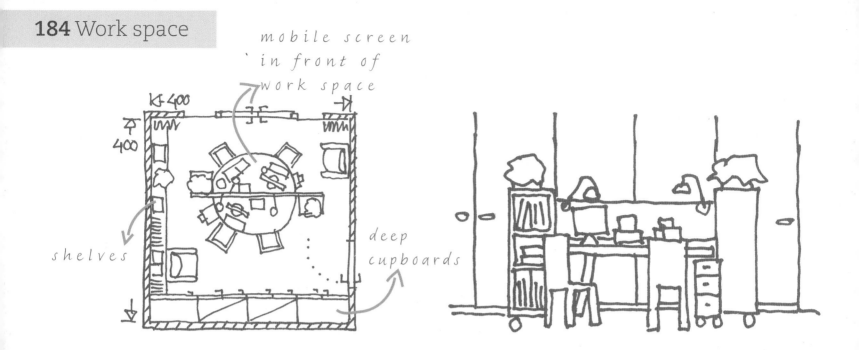

drawers   cupboards/cabinets

seating

300

work desk   475

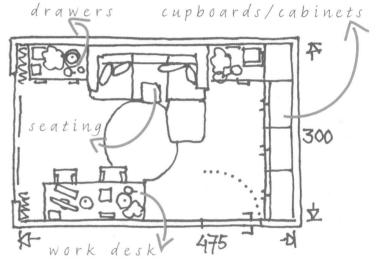

wall units

450

350

cupboard

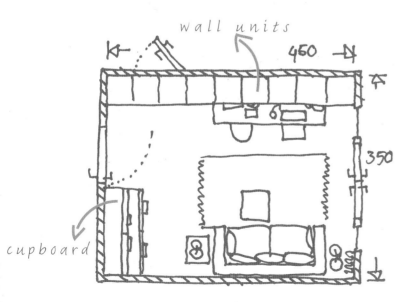

Work space layout

You can work anywhere, as long as there is enough storage space. A round table with a screen across the middle and with two shelving units attached on either side provides two work spaces, or one work space and a dining area. Chests of drawers either side of a sofa, and a tension wire with clips for photographs and notes keep papers in order. A wall unit from floor to ceiling, either side of the door and desk, keeps files and folders out of sight.

Chapter 8

The attic

Beneath the roof's sloping eaves lies a place of shelter. A safe place to sleep, work or play – and whatever else besides. Here, there is room for cosiness, intimacy and atmosphere. It would be a shame to use the attic only for storage.

Laid out with love
and attention: a
fully-fledged room
high up in the rafters

Wish list

- *integral part of the home*
- *organization*
- *insulation*
- *light and space*

Integral part of the home
The attic deserves more than being designated a dusty, dark space for storage. It is a flexible space with a wealth of possibilities: spare room, bedroom, study, second living room or playroom. Arrange the space carefully to turn the attic into an integral aspect of your home with every bit as much style and ambience. You could even turn it into a miniature apartment, including shower and kitchenette for longer term guests. Keep it all cheerful and light.

Organization
Obviously the attic is the place above all others for keeping the things that you seldom or never use. But do not just dump things such as your camping equipment, skis, roller blades, old stereo equipment and vinyl record collection in the attic without a second thought. Put them on shelves, custom-built to fit between sloping walls. Incorporate your own wall units with doors under the roof. Let them reach only halfway up to the apex and set the head of a bed against them, giving you a sort of bedside table effect on either side.

Insulation
Insulate the attic to keep outside cold or heat at bay. You can insert insulation material between the beams – if the beams are worth keeping on view. Fitting insulation under the roof tiles is more laborious and expensive. The cheapest and easiest solution is to fit insulation material over the beams, which is what you should do if you want to create an uninterrupted, level ceiling.

Light and space
If possible, remove all dividing walls. Paint everything white. Possibly, include a dormer window. You could also add a hint of colour to white paint, such as pale pink or blue, to create a subtle warmth or glow. Blue creates an illusion of depth and is all the more appropriate as a colour considering that in the attic you are, after all, right beneath the sky itself.

!idea

You could convert the attic into a guest apartment, complete with its own shower and kitchenette. This 'loft apartment' idea is bound to tempt you, too. Could you resist using it sometimes as your retreat beneath the eaves?

First published in 2003 as a VT Wonen publication entitled
Woon by Sanoma Uitgevers B.V.
Capellalaan 65, 2132 JL Hoofddorp,
Netherlands
© Sanoma Uitgevers Hoofddorp 2003

This edition published in 2005 by Conran Octopus Limited
a part of Octopus Publishing Group
2–4 Heron Quays, London E14 4JP
www.conran-octopus.co.uk

Editor-in-Chief Makkie Mulder

Art directors Janine Couperus, Madelon Vink

Image coordination and composition Heleen van Gent

Text Juliette Berkhout

Final editing Annemieke van Twuijver

Illustrations Frans Bramlage, Madelon Vink

Line-extension coordinator Mieke Beljaarts

Project editor Linda Pijper

Photography Jan Baldwin, Alexander van Berge, Maurice
Brands, Dennis Brandsma, John Dummer, Hotze Eisma,
Luuk Geertsen, Simone de Geus, Paul Grootes, Guiba
Guimarâes, Per Gunnarson, Ewout Huibers, Eline Klein,
Peter Kooijman, Anneke de Leeuw, Louis Lemaire, Erik van
Lokven, Otto Polman, Femke Reijerman, Robert Sledwinski,
Joyce Vloet, Hans Zeegers

Styling Nina Monfils (coordination), Yvonne Bakker, Julia
Bird, Frans Bramlage, Fietje Bruijn, Irene de Coninck, Nans
van Dam, Désiree van Dijk, Cirina 't Hart, Mirjam Huygens,
Sylvie Jones, Kristel de Jong, Esther Jostmeijer, Jet Krings,
Linda Loenen, Marianne Luning, Gentia Luyckx, Corry
Nowee, Monique Postma, Jacqueline Roeleveld, Mirjam
Roskamp, Mirella Sahetapy, Mirabelle Scheelings, Olga
Serrarens, Reini Smit, Frans Uyterlinde, Petra de Valk,
Nicolette de Waart, Jolanda Wassenaar, Valerie van der Werff

Responsibility for the design of kitchens and bathrooms:
Piet Boon
Oostzaan, +31 (0)75-6843656 (page 81 above right, 108)
Eckhardt & Leeuwenstein
Amsterdam, +31 (0)20-6261340 (page 67, 94)
Jan van Erp
Kaatsheuvel, +31 (0)416-279039 (page 144)
Foucault
Waspik, +31 (0)416-315820 (page 82, 83)
Keukenhuys De Tweede Kamer
Kaatsheuvel, +31 (0)416-274747 (page 107 below left)
Lodder Keukens
Barneveld, +31 (0)342-422370 (page 80, 81 above left, 89, 103)
Soap Ateliers
Rotterdam, +31 (0)10-2210866 (page 86, 88, 96, 97 below
centre, 133 below centre, 136, 138, 139)
Wim de Vos
Amsterdam, +31 (0)20-6232624 (page 132, 133 above centre)

Other kitchens were designed by VT Wonen stylists
in conjunction with various kitchen suppliers
and manufacturers.

With thanks to Michèle Coebergh, Carla Happee, Janneke
Staats, Manon Suykerbuyk. Special thanks are due to all those
who allowed VT Wonen the use of their interiors and to
everyone photographed in this book.

Publisher Peter Schönhuth

Printing coordination Mieke Dekker, Mark van der Ham

Lithography Litho Spirit

Printed by MKT Print d. d. Ljubljana

UK Edition translated by Guy Shipton for First Edition
Translations Limited

Jacket Design Victoria Burley

British Library Cataloguing-in-Publication Data. A catalogue
record for this book is available from the British Library.

ISBN 1 84091 426 2